salmonpoetry

Skip Diving
Celeste Augé

Published in 2014 by
Salmon Poetry
Cliffs of Moher, County Clare, Ireland
Website: www.salmonpoetry.com
Email: info@salmonpoetry.com

ISBN 978-1-908836-88-5

COVER IMAGE: "Raingirl" by Joan Sugrue – www.joansugrue.com
COVER DESIGN & TYPESETTING: *Siobhán Hutson*
Printed in Ireland by Sprint Print

*Salmon Poetry gratefully acknowledges the support of
The Arts Council / An Chomhairle Ealaoín*

Acknowledgments

My thanks to the editors of the following publications, where some of these poems first appeared:

Dogs Singing: A Tribute Anthology, ed. Jessie Lendennie, Salmon Poetry, Cliffs of Moher, 2010
Cúirt Journal, Issue Number 5, ed. Charlie McBride, Stonebridge Publications, 1998
Skylight 47, Issue 1, Winter 2013
Burning Bush 2, Issue Number 4, January 2013
Abridged 0-28, Once a Railroad, 2013
Blue Max Review, 2013
Dromineer Literary Festival website, October 2013
The Honest Ulsterman, Issue 2, 2014

I am extremely grateful to the Arts Council for the granting of a Literature Bursary that allowed me to work on a substantial part of this poetry collection. Thanks are also due to the Galway County Arts Office for their generous sponsorship of a stay in the Tyrone Guthrie Centre, where some of these poems were conceived.

Special thanks to Sheila and Elaine for being astute first readers of my manuscript; to Dani Gill and everyone at Cúirt for their support; to Moya, Aoife and Lorna for the poetry chat; to all my friends (assorted writers, engineers, cake-makers, skivvies, SNAs, teachers, dreamers and rogues) for putting up with me throughout the writing of these poems.

Contents

The Cool October Sunshine

reminds you of the time you were walking through the Botanic Gardens—amongst the young mothers and fathers pushing their squawking buggies, foreign grey squirrels diving across the path, the two lads sipping Dutch Gold on a fallen tree trunk on the other side of the Tolka River (discussing what they would do differently if they were in charge), sculptures and rich autumn blooms turned towards the sun—and you couldn't resist the impulse to peel off your teal blue cardigan, frilled blue blouse and matching skirt, your flats and tights, your comfortable underwear dropped onto the alpines, so that you joined the trees in their autumn bare-ness, skin prickling against the cold, arms outstretched, tall as the specimen trees, your skin mottled purple and white, the trunk of a new breed of tree, *arbor femina*, a small black plaque following your swift feet as you skirt the hills of Glasnevin, not looking for anything—oh shame the devil and tell the truth!—looking for the life you once lived here, your own naked ghost, skinny, narrow-hipped, the girl who once looked for you, the stripped bare life you have now. Look, you would say to her (May's daughter, Winnie's granddaughter, cultivated from a long line of peasant farmers), this is all you ever needed: your whole self and your appreciation of quiet, of an inappropriate laugh, knowing that when you open your mouth, marbles and seashells and granite stones—jagged ones—will spill out. Forget the show of spring leaves you missed. You're an October girl—bare yourself.

Because Not All Truths

Because not all truths
can be subjected to scientific scrutiny
and survive in any shape
that approximates their spirit
I will not ask why
you have put up with me
all these hormonal years,
nor why in the face of sense
you love me—not once asking me
to stop talking while you read,
never wondering what I'm thinking
when the storm clouds roll in
nor looking for sense from me
when words take me over.
I will step back, I will forego
the microscope (this time)
and I will stretch my life out
alongside yours, as though we're
two teenagers lying back in the grass,
going nowhere, growing invisibly
as we watch the clouds change
from Felix the Cat to a tree stump
to a cow to the shape of a shell
and the crab that lives in it.

Oh Canada

Oh Canada
my home and native land
I can't say I miss you, I'm not sure I know you.
I remember your frogs (we used to race them),
washboard laughs on the way to the dump,
garter snakes, blueberries in burnt woods,
building tunnels under your ice-crusted snow.
The way you chased me from season to season—
from slush to mosquito fogs to crunchy leaves
to tongue-sticky handrails.

Oh Canada
I remember when
they changed your song in Grade Two.
I can sing part of the second stanza in French,
but the rest of your anthem has gone
the way of the friends I played with in Kindergarten
and the stink from the mill stack that floated up
our hill. I never got to know your cities.

Oh Canada
you remind me of my dad.
Always wanting to go somewhere else,
be someone else, better, work harder, quiet.
Be nice. Don't get ahead of yourself,
don't get a big head, figure it out first,
make sure you have the right tools.
Câline de bine and guff and the friggin moose
that wrecked our windshield
the week before we left for good.

Oh Canada
I don't know where I belong
or where the field I grew up in is gone
or how to become you
when I'm not even sure who you are now
or why I have mapped you across my back.
Maybe that's as close as I can keep you.

My Dad Visits After Twenty Years of Silence

We talk about cars;
who's driving what,
which parts don't work,

speculate that the world's
wars could be ended
with the demise of
the Toyota Hilux pickup—

now there's a reliable truck,
get you and your buddies, some
guns, safely across the desert
or around mountains
or past jungles (and juntas)
ready to battle another day.

A real guy car, we agree,
a real guy car.

Friday

Today is Friday and I'm out of metaphors—
the wind howling though the trees outside
is just the wind that knocks down the wheelie bin
which is just a bin blown over that scatters
egg cartons, yoghurt pots and plastic bottles
over the gravel stones outside my house
that are simply stones (though a lot of them)
and my house is a house, rectangular,
white, four walls and a roof, nothing more.
This pen I hold writes only words—blue words.
As in the colour blue.

Somewhere else a five-year-old boy picks up
a fragment of a cluster bomb (where it might
be windy, too)—they aren't metaphors
either (neither the boy nor the bomb).
My own son is with my neighbour,
(somewhere out there in a black Ford)
both of them flesh and bone, representing
themselves (their best and their worst selves).
I sit here and I mean nothing more than
woman sitting on a couch on a Friday afternoon
writing and waiting.

Quiet

When I am quiet

I hear the birds pass their chirps
to each other

the wind graze the trees
outside my window

electricity hum through
the fluorescent bulb

your bare feet plod on
the distant kitchen floor

I hear your breath——I hear your chest
rise and fall

my ears buzz with the steady
riff of you

Gym Poem #1

Tracksuit

My muscles and tendons stitch along my bones
like a comfortable tracksuit that knows the shape of me,
my life, the limited shapes of the work I do.

Weekend Alone

You know you're bored—even lonely,
and don't forget procrastinating—
when some guy from Meteor
customer service rings your phone,
says his name is Musheer
and you actually write it down.
He sounds as if he's next door,
he sounds as if he's far away.

'Do you have a few minutes
to discuss your experience of Meteor?'
And you do, you take your time
answering, trying to be accurate.
'Any other comments?' he asks,
but while you're thinking how
he could be right next door,
he could be far, far away

'Anything else we can do for you?'
pops out of the phone. 'Yes,'
you say. You aren't waiting this time.
'Where are you from, Musheer?'
A pause. 'And where are you now?'
Silence. You guess this isn't in his script.
'It's raining here in Galway,' you add,
'it's lashing against the door.'

You picture him amidst the phones,
thinking weather thoughts.
The voices around him buzz away.
'It's raining here in Bangalore,'
he says, 'it's raining here, too!'
A grin beams from phone to phone,
makes you feel he's just next door,
makes you feel far away.

Stop the Lights

Next time I'll go straight to drunk—
I'll bypass scrubbing the toilet,
moving the furniture around,
making sure there are enough chairs
for everyone I have invited.

Stop the lights, I want to yell,
stop the lights right there! I'm too old
to watch my prodigal father try to woo
my mother twenty-five years after
he left, founded a new family.

Unwavering, she looks up over
her reading glasses, flirts when she fancies
and the rest of the time, ignores him.
This is her life, her money,
her daughters and grandson.

The lights focus on the pair of them.
He leans in close to her, grabs her attention,
arm across the back of her chair.
She calls over her grandson, distraction.
Tomorrow, she'll have my father drive her

across Connemara. They'll go to lunch,
relive old times. Maybe argue a bit.
This is a game they are playing out
I tell myself and my two sisters
as we get drunk on gift wine,

dance around the kitchen singing
'Firework' and 'I Will Survive'.
It's not our show, we chant,
this mess is their life and we're just
here for the party, shimmying

to our own reunion; we are like
showgirls on the last night of a long run—
high kicks and no underwear
for the heck of it—dancing away
from our parents' past, trying

to abandon that dead lump of life
under the borrowed table and chairs
on the living room floor—at the feet
of our seventy-something parents—
as we dance into our own
                          glorious mistakes.

Ode

'More happy love! more happy, happy love!
Forever warm and still to be enjoy'd...'
    —JOHN KEATS, *Ode on a Grecian Urn*

You lie across my thighs as I write,
my bone-warming hot water bottle,
pure latex, guaranteed to delight the most
discriminating women, mottle their thighs
as they lie deep in their beds, pretending
this rubber sack of warm water
could never replace their lover.

The women of Ireland drive with you
across their laps, hand-knit covers
helping to keep you warm. More love,
the patterns passed down from
mothers and grandmothers, still enjoyed.
They knit covers for each new bottle,
battle the cold, inside and out.

Every woman remembers her first.
I was twelve, three hours after landing
in Ireland, in Granny's front bedroom.
You are the best invention after
hot water on tap, and when old age hits
and you warm through rheumatism—
not period pains—I hope to bits
I will have more to hug than my hottle
(Granny's word for hot water bottle).

Women Improve With the Years

after Yeats

I am worn out with diets—
those rain-worn, concrete goddesses
among the skinny streets.
All winter long I look at magazines
and try out each new fad
I find in each new book.
Pretending: I am a future beauty, too.
But I'm pleased with myself,
to have the power of all four limbs,
eyes that can read the headlines, a body
that has grown a baby, loved on a whim.
Women improve with the years;
I switch on the light, don't mind
who sees my stretch marks. If we meet
at my burning age, watch out! I grow
ludic in the rain—a diet-worn, fleshy
goddess at play among the shops.

On Nature

Nature has nothing to do with me.
Nature has everything to do with me.

Outside my window, the clouds blow past.
Fast rain howls down, will
fill the drains, top up
over the doorsills in town.

Nature has nothing to do with me.
Rain empties into the wheelie bin
in the middle of my living room—
nature has everything to do with me.

Leaves fall, and they block more drains.
Plain November. The air becomes still.
Nature has little to do with us.
Loved ones pass and their souls do too.

Nature has nothing to do with us.
Days shorten to grey. More people leave.
Previous floods freeze. The taps freeze.
Nature has everything to do with us.

Water

Quiet.
Turn off the television.
Switch off the power
at the breaker.
Take your children

and get to higher ground.
Rush each step. Listen.
Shump.
Whoosh.
Creak.

This is how it sounds
when your house
is ripped up
and all your possessions
float away.

Earth Studies: Killaguile

Cillín. 115339E 238890N. 24 November 2011.

From one square metre of ground
I dig and find:
a fox's black scat, rainwater
collected in the chipped rim of a saucer,
quaking-grass and couch-grass
in amongst the common bent grass,
an earring with three small fake pearls,
haircap moss on a fallen birch branch,
a red fairy stool. Deep-brown peat,
the same colour as the limb of oak it has preserved,
and stretched out alongside that, a tiny human femur.
The tangle of a cep's hair-like mycelium
anointing a four-day-old mute hyoid bone.
Any number of dew-worms.
Three pairs of foetal lunate bones without
the digits that once bloomed from them.
Seventeen common rough woodlice
huddled under a decomposing branch.
The peat-filled skull of an Irish hare.
A thatch of bark, still growing lichen.
The pottery handle of what seems to have been a jug.
A palmful of the smallest auditory ossicles imaginable—
hammers, anvils, stirrups bumping randomly
against each other, transferring
the sound of soil and bone.
Birch leaves and beech leaves in various states of decay.
Granite stones.
Placeless infant clavicles, miscarried skulls with
undescended teeth, mandibles, pocket-sized ribs, vertebrae.
One small strip of torn linen, a loop at one end.
Minute humeri, capulae, ulnae.
A perfectly black ground beetle burrowing even deeper.

Unidentified baby phalanges, patellae, tibiae and fibulae.
Unidentified larvae.
The silence of the men who came late at night
to bury their impure babies.
A flake of my own skin, to prove that I was here.

Carrying Water

in memory of my grandmother, Winnie Fahy (née Bohan)

It takes three litres of water
to flush the upstairs toilet.
Five litres to wash up after dinner.

I quickly learnt these amounts
carrying water from my neighbour's house
the winter the pipes froze.

Granny would have laughed at my panic—
when will the thaw come, will we have enough
water for the morning, don't empty
that hot water bottle down the drain,
I'll use it in the cistern, when will the thaw come—

she who carried buckets filled with water
over the hill, enough for three babies
under five years, never mind the others,
day in, day out.
                    Let no one say
she went to bed at night without leaving
clean water in the house,
or that she wouldn't have a spare bucketful
by the back door in case someone stopped by.

Open house:
she'd have the neighbours in, Chevasse,
the Master or the vagrant storyteller-drunk.

She kept up tradition without wanting to—
part midwife, part farmer, part mother.
Time didn't even come into it.

Electricity and running water came
when all nine children had left.
She could listen to a dance on the radio,
draw a bath, wash the delph in the damp
back kitchen. Front door always open,
windows clean, otherwise

what would people think?

Doesn't Every Woman?

Doesn't every woman pile her bills, her to-do lists, her
 unread books in the middle of the kitchen table?
Pile her washing on the comfiest armchair?
Pile her clutter into the spare room when her friends call
 over?

Sweep her rage under the bed to join the dust bunnies?

Howl at the moon, or if the moon isn't working, at the
 nearest patch of testosterone (or her mother, if she's
 still around)?

Know how to perform a straight-arm takedown?
Know how to crochet a granny square? How to roller
 skate? How to play 'It's Raining Men' on the ukulele?

Cry at the start of *Bambi*, at the start of *Up*, through the
 last twenty minutes of *Beaches*?
Cry when she can't figure out how to do it all, or any
 of it, really?
Cry at the thought of her mother dying or her friends
 leaving?

Wish her mother would stop giving her advice or start
 giving her useful advice (like how to choose the
 winning numbers)? Or that her mother would listen
 to her; for once take *her* advice?

Wish she could work and stay at home at the same time?
Get fed up of needing to be two of herself?

Wish all the other women would join her, storm
 government buildings and corporate headquarters and
 rip those grey suits off the men in power, let them
 rule nude? Wish the men would just hand over the
 keys to the world, let us figure it out for a while?

Wish all the world's religions would butt out and stop telling her what to do with her hair, womb, mind, clitoris, hands?

Keep her hems up with safety pins?

Try to pin her lover to the bed when she's fertile and aching or futile and hungry?

Hire a kango hammer to wake up the neighbours?

Daydream when she's studying or cleaning or meeting her boss for her quarterly review?
Laugh out loud at the jokes inside her head when she's studying or cleaning or meeting her boss for her quarterly review?

Eat an entire packet of biscuits on Friday?

Feel like she's still ten (and ready to rule the world)?
Feel like she's still nineteen (and ready to convict the world)?
Feel like she's still too young to know what to be when she grows up?

Always wear concealer, even in bed?
Grow a five o'clock shadow when she runs out of wax?
Keep her depression in her sock drawer?

Keep an emergency bottle of guilt in with her clean knickers?
Keep an emergency dark chocolate Kit Kat in the top drawer next to her bed?
Stay in the shower for longer than it takes to get clean, just to feel the water running over her breasts, her belly, her thighs?

Do the dusting in her comfie underpants when
  everyone's gone out?
Dance around the house singing 'R.E.S.P.E.C.T.' at the
  top of her voice?
Leave her dirty dishes around the house?
Prefer toast and tea in bed?
Crave chocolate at least once a month? Once a day?
Once an hour?
Love cheese-and-onion crisps with chocolate?
Love a good love scene?
Love the word 'discombobulate'?
Love at least one man in her lifetime?
Eventually love her feet?
Love her redundant parents and love her wandering
  children?
Love her thoughts?
Love her talk?
Love her dreams?

Doesn't every woman dream?

After the election

we feel cleansed,
shiny with the final count,
with what we might do,
the buildings we might scour
of cronies and money
passed with handshakes
and in-fighting

as though old Ireland
will be cleansed
by the change of suit
the way the city's grimy streets
are new again—ion-filled—
after a good three days
of hard rain.

Clean Up

On 11/2/2011, eighteen days of public protest in Tahrir Square ended when Egypt's dictator President Hosni Mubarak resigned after nearly thirty years in power.

On the nineteenth day, text messages
call the protesters back to the Square.

They arrive with brooms, mops and buckets,
gloves, and signs taped their chests—

Sorry for the disturbance, we're building Egypt.
They sweep Cairo's streets,

gather up the rubbish, scrub graffiti.
Mohammed says they'll take care of the Square,

then they'll clean up the whole country,
brush the dust off, purify the past,

polish their monuments and kerbsides,
their sense of self. Start clean.

The people of Egypt are changing themselves
to become their new country

while we, the anxious world, watch for more news,
twitching net curtains in rooms freshly cleaned

to welcome guests from the other
side of the powerless sea.

Deepwater Horizon Widow

I didn't get to clean his body.
Eleven men float through the sea,
cells buffeted by tide and swell.

He lives in the ocean now
with the heavily-oiled pelicans
and the slick leatherback turtles.

Oil swirls near the ocean floor,
coral reefs unlit, smothered
as the oil floats up to terns, blue herons,

egrets and spoonbills.
I volunteer to clean up,
pluck a tern from the basin,

clamp its bill and slide my hand
down its side, vegetable soap
cutting through raw oil.

The motion of my hand cleaning
soothes neither of us.
My arm coils around the tern's

now-frizzy body and it starts
to struggle, as if instinct awakens
and it knows it will survive,

neck straining against my grasp
towards the sea,
the desire to return home.

Mess

for my mother

Dirty dishes pile up on the floor,
sorted into categories
only she understands,
on temporary newspaper rugs.
The Advertiser, usually.
Old copies of *Alive!* stack up
in the corner next to the plant
she's nursing back to vigour.

She hasn't yet got around
to replacing the shattered glass
of the oven door, she hangs
a striped tea towel over it.
There's always a chance
she'll move again, anyway.

Over her shoulder, she glimpses
her mother walk in,
all these years after her death.
She missed her chance
to tell her, yes, she understood,
they both did the best they could.
Emptied the thatch house
of her childhood every Saturday,
scrubbed it bare, as if secrets
could be removed like a stain.

She senses her mother start to fuss.
'This is my mess,' she says.
'Stop worrying. I know
where the important things are.
One of these days, I'll find
a place for everything.'

Absolution

I, too, have sinned,
in several different religions.
(Roast pork, assorted blasphemies,
not to mention the fornication.)

For me, doing the laundry offers
neither penance nor money
nor the dead certainty of the same view
in the same stone house
for the rest of my life.

I'm trying to wash away the stains
of another pointless argument,
another dig and drag down to the level of
you never pick up your underpants
or *it's not my turn to make lunch.*

But the yellow marks won't shift
out of either shirt—my favourite blouse,
your special occasion cuffs.

What were we even fighting about?
I regret picking up that American mustard,
squeezing the bottle, hard—my flash temper
getting the worst of me again—

now here I am, up to my elbows in suds.
*Sure, blame it on the Americans,
isn't it always their fault,*
your voice in my head

and I'm laughing,
and like that I can't wait to see
your broad face across the table tonight,
your warm outline in bed.

Miracles Are For Anyone Who Believes

We're coming up to Christmas
and I need something to believe in
to get me through the winter lows.

The lit windows are a constellation
traced across the roads out here.
Memories appear in the half-light,

trip me up, make me wonder
if I turn down the wrong road tonight
will there be a door open for me?

If every marvel on this road
could be given a shape in lights,
the sky would pale till

I could walk the low road,
be led to my own front door
by a hoar-frost of miracles

suspended in mid-air.

Prayers and Crumbs Can Only Get You So Far

Normally I wouldn't be out this late
(maybe to the gate, to check the dog went)
where each house becomes a dusk island
joined hand to hand by a fine filament,
an empty tin at either end
so we can hear each other's voice,
ask for a lift in the morning,
warn of roaming cattle or black ice,
live in the belief of a fire
in the grate, the wire that transmits
my neighbour's voice, toast dripping
with butter and your hand holding it.

Forgotten

By the time I come out the other end of this life,
  will I have forgotten
  how it felt to be three,
the humble buzz of bees moving from clover flowers
to buttercups the same height as me,
the taste of freshly hand-dug gravel,
and the way a black beetle scuttles
  between my bare feet;

how close I was then to the start of things,
my skin permeable, holding nothing out,
everything I could touch or see, mine—
no, not mine, but a part of me—

  ready to be stroked or taken apart?

I Hope My First Death
Will Be Gentle

There are too many ways to die.
The number ten bus, rushing off to Belfield.
Some young buck in a pimped-up Honda Civic.
My unpredictable heart, giving up mid-line.
Or the drag of cancer, my breath faltering,
the nurse—a stranger, really—healing me
with a final elixir,
        annointing me secretly
           (a few drops over the measure),
             granting me the integrity
              of my life.

Girlhood

A little girl in green boots
moves the beach around
to suit her—channels tidewater
the way she wants it to go,
builds walls out of wet sand
and soft-edge stones,
turns the water's progress
sideways, and blocks it
halfway down to the surf—
because the beach is hers,
because she can.

Voyeur

Flicking through years, I watch myself
and my sisters dig a hole
in the sandy edge of the driveway,
smooth girl-faces bent down,
oblivious that we'll ever be watched.

The others come back from the untended field,
empty their pockets into the large hole
until the last squirming toad has been dumped.
My young self grabs a shovel.
The ground is dry and full of stones;
easy to scrape the hole back in—quick!—
over the pit of dry toads.

We stand back, admire our work.
Wait. See if the toads can tunnel
their way out from the earth. Bored
waiting, we'll dig the ground back out,
toad-legs flying past our girl-legs
as the shovel shows no mercy.

Skip Diving

in memory of my Aunt Bridgie

I pinch my nose, bend my legs
and sploosh, plunge straight into
this vast yellow skip, head first,
my feet flapping hopelessly
against the chipped floral set
of porcelain mugs that she picked up
in Royal Tara's closing down sale,
graze my ankle by the edge
of her glass worktop saver.
I blink through cobwebs, descend past
terracotta pots and dead arecas,
past battery chargers, plugboards,
two pairs of lamps, glasses,
knives, forks and spoons,
a good heavy butcher's block
and a barely-used George Foreman Grill.
A Tube ticket from the morning she retired.
Old mortgage papers and even older
divorce papers, community mission statements,
a scrunched-up till receipt from Ryans
for a coat she could almost afford.
I anchor my fingertips on a Child of Prague,
pull myself past a handwoven Bridget's Cross,
a clock that will chime a different
bird call on the hour, skim right past
the copper immersion tank to reach the books,
the wool blanket Granny crocheted,
and the cushion embroidered:
'Home Is Where the Arguments Are'.

I, who never liked to swim, dive
down, try to salvage an entire woman
from the remnants of her life—

dumped out the back of her house—
try to salvage the times we laughed
at each other and the infinite crazy world,
the long chats we wasted on winter days
in front of the turf-burning range.

Against the pressure in my lungs, I dive
right down to the family secrets,
passed on to her for safe-keeping—
secrets as ordinary or devastating
or perfect as any family's—
hold in the single gasp of memory
that will take me back to the surface
behind her barren house.

The Secret Keepers

You can spot us because we hold
our hands over our mouths,
even when we laugh—to keep things
in or out, I don't know—or else
we hold our hands at our sides, or
in our pockets, wherever feels right.
Sometimes we let slip the names
of our mothers or our neighbours.
We fear that revealing whatever
secret has been planted inside us
means spontaneous combustion
(think fires of hell) or something worse.
We imagine our whole world caving in,
kitchen floors plummeting, chair legs
splintered, broken tiles everywhere,
waving our arms from a black hole
and not a helping hand to grasp.

Washing

Bleach them in the sunlight:
white cotton undies, nighties, pillowcases
strung out across the garden,
waving in a gentle breeze.

Take them inside—
air-dried, stiff, smelling of pollen—
fold that familiar bundle
into neat piles, put them away
safe, where they belong.

Why do you pawn things rather than sell?

Karen said:

Because I want them back—
I want the chance
to get them back—

I just want a chance.

The world doesn't owe me
anything but
it owes me a chance.

Ghost

Granddad sits on the front lawn, rocking.
As long as Granddad sits there
in his rocking chair we will be safe.
He flickers in the sun, waiting.

Meanwhile, inside the house, we too wait.
Hide behind the couch. Waiting
for the mortgage owners,
for the house to be whisked away.

Our neighbours don't know.
We talk smaller and smaller. The gap
between our houses grows.

The House That Peter Built

1

It's the way she hides her laugh
    behind her hand
that makes him fall rock hard
    in love with her.
She walks down the road past
    his mother's house
in skirts, dresses, petticoats; he watches
    her fledge girlhood.
He nods to her in the market, lifts
    his cap, head down—
he'll wait until the stone slates
    cover the roof
to find out how her voice sounds
    up against
his first (and only) question.

Her name is Bridget. She's the one.
    He gets to work.

2

The house weathers grey, develops
    mould on top of mould.
Windows gape at the changing view
    no one looks out at
from an empty room next to another
    empty room.
Blocks laid so carefully by hand that
    not one has shifted
against the tangle of brambles growing
    up around
the virgin house. This is the house
    of desire, a folly

we will drive past for over fifty years
     until some young man
takes it in hand, glazes the windows,
     mounts a Sky dish,
fits the first lock the house
     has ever needed.

Mixtape Poem

The last time you heard that song
was on a mixtape Constance gave you;
when you thought adulthood was a long
word away. Thursday night meant a bong
and a few cans before you'd hit Xanadu's.
Time flew. Last you heard, that song
meant good-bye and good-luck, you were wrong
to think fun would go on forever. Screw
all the mixtapes Constance ever gave you,
that was decades ago, the lust should be gone.
A wife, three kids, two dogs, a rat (almost a zoo!)
since the last time you had a theme song
taped for you. Now you google chicks in thongs,
she-males and cheap flights, thrills from blue
flicks on tapes some fella gives you.
'Don't tell my wife,' after *Bonking King Kong*.
Swing shifts, school runs, footie. Who knew
adulthood would crash along like a mixtape,
that over and over you'd hear the same songs.

Flat-packers

1

And the arguments clang
between the shelves
of barely-contained rage—
brown cardboard boxes
mosh down the aisles—
tannoy calls for co-workers
to clean up the mess left
in Aisle 25 Location 13—
the contents of an abandoned trolley
scattered on the screed
beneath Hemnes, Edland, Leksvik.

2

It is the look of abandonment,
the heart-shaped cushion clutched
to her chest, its stitched-on arms
flopping—useless—on either side of her,
that drives Michael to it.

'Now are you happy?' he says,
clenches the bulbous pink plastic stool,
reaches back, deep breath,
and they both wonder if
he's going to fling it—

heel-toe shift
    one step
        release
            the stool flies
                past shallow boxes
                    past herds of people

and it clips dodging staff,
ankle-high—three down—
ricochets on past Expedit,
past Liatorp, takes down displays
of plastic watering cans, cushions,
stacks of floppy soft mats;

pure energy bounding
up the stairs into the showrooms,
bounces off every natty couch,
gathers momentum from the crackle
of Trish versus Mike—
'Do you not realise we need a Besta?'
and 'We'll never fit that in the boot
even if we put the seats down
and the flipping baby in your lap!'—

uses the accumulated energy
of one hundred concurrent rows
to fly through each display
in this vast warehouse of rooms
without windows or doors
as he sparks and she sparks into life
over the necessary components
of their ideal bookcase.

Universal Uterus

Sealed into the vacuum pack of family
you wait for a balanced system to emerge.
You're available. You're their urgent
care and 24-hour superstore.
They go to the other side of the glass dome
for a couple of hours, to give you 'space',
but call twelve times in three hours.

CO2 levels start to soar, dissolve into
the salt pond, eat the coral reef.
Tiny mites attack the crops and you have
less and less to eat. At night you switch
the kitchen lights out—millions of cockroaches
cover every surface. No one can come in
or go out. You're an experiment in systems.

You wait for balance. The oxygen starts
to disappear. You're suffocating, slowly.
And now you end up spitting in each
other's faces. Fights over where the oxygen
is going. Then millions of ants appear
from nowhere, wage war on the roaches.
You watch food move across the floor.

This wasn't how it was supposed to be.
You had dreams. The ants win, destroy
the cockroaches, eat through the silicone
seal that secures your world, and march off
into the oblivious desert; while you watch
and wonder how long you'd last
if you followed them.

Lost Fathers

One day they're here, next thing they're gone.
Tools abandoned in the shed, their best suit left
for someone to grow into. Soon, they're as good
as dead. They exist only in the past tense
(same as their own dead fathers).

Years and years later—before they're forgotten—
they invent different ways of returning.

They sidle up the side steps of a courthouse, or
they glide in on parachutes or an open-top bus.

They open their arms wide.

When they're not holding their arms out,
they place their hands on their chest, say sorry.

They talk about all the things they've done since
they last saw you, prepare a slideshow—
at least one hundred photos—show you the other
children they have raised in other places.

They talk a lot. They have many years
of speechlessness to make up for.

They show how they've mellowed.
They rarely shout now, and haven't pitched
a dinner plate in years.

They steel themselves for the worst.
Possible armour:
an open return ticket, an itemised list
of all the wrongs done to them,
an itemised list of all their bills and expenses,

an impenetrable layer of sunscreen, bug
repellent and aftershave, a hearing aid
with a volume switch they can turn down,
the ability to laugh at anyone.

They stay as long as it takes to find
their other self, the tracks they left behind
in the city of their youth. They walk the streets
and lanes until their backs start to hurt.

Always Sligo Rovers

for Shea and Sam

The ancestors at Garavogue Villas
don't care that we can't pay the rent.
Their stone circle is still here, disguised
as a roundabout. Lichen covers the stones.
In the middle, the Blessed Virgin Mary—
in an all-white strip—protects the ancestors,
prays over them, right on the spot
where their bones used to lie.
Their 5,000-year-old tomb is gone.
Parked cars hide the touchline
where we used to play kerbs. Sometimes,
late at night, I pass Whitewash Mary,
always praying, always quiet,
that half smile playing around her lips,
her curves dimly lit by streetlights—
lone mother of the night—and I want
to kick the stray football to her, shout:
'Get up to it, Mary, nod it back!'

At the Showgrounds, the mountains surround us,
ancestors everywhere—on Knocknarea,
Keelogboy, the Ballygawley Hills, Ben Bulben.
The sky is thick with ancestors—
there isn't too far you can go in this town
without someone knowing what you're
up to. Bohs are in with a chance but
we've got Joseph Ndo who brings
a kind of stillness to every pass of the ball,
as though he's surrounded by a different
type of air, the ancestors at his feet.
And sometimes when it's a good night
in the Showgrounds and no one
has cursed the result, that same kind

of force field hovers right around the grounds,
around the signs for Tohers and Jako,
energy conjured up by the ancestors—
who else could it be?—watching over us.

A minute's silence for the ancestors, for their
protection, everyone up on their feet,
a minute's silence for any help the ancestors
might give tonight, the night when
Rovers line out against Bohs, the night when
Uncle S brings his newly-fatherless nephew
to see his first match in the Showgrounds,
when Google brings his future wife to see
what she's letting herself in for, when
Seamus brings his young son to the only place
on earth where he will be allowed
to swear loudly at each lost tackle, wrong penalty,
missed chance, the ancestors watching over them,
that blessed moment before the whistle blows,
a moment's silence, please,
                              and we remember
our pasts, our people returned to us for tonight—
as though their spirits could come back to earth,
touch down right there on the pitch.

Postcards From Home

It's harder to be the one left behind, gaps left
where your friend or sister used to stand.

Gaps you can't walk into, or brush past
without displacing one more speck of them,

to be vacuumed up on a Friday morning.
Until not one iota of the one you love,

the one who left, remains in the spaces
you fought over (the remote control,

the TV chair, the downstairs toilet,
the stool up at the bar next to the taps),

until you can't see the spaces you should
be stepping around, and you can't help but

step right on the spot where Catríona
used to wait for a pint of Heineken, and say

have you heard from Catríona lately, strange
name on your tongue, distant as though

you have changed channels, are watching
a different soap now.

Gym Poem #2

The Annual Graveside Mass for the Departed

This isn't another ghost poem.
This is a poem where the voices
drifting in from the cemetery
belong to the people gathered outside
for this year's graveyard mass.

This is a poem where I run out of breath
rowing to nowhere on a Concept 2,
where another woman takes it out
on a treadmill instead of her three sons
and where the old guy (who nearly
walks off the end his treadmill)
gets dragged here by his wife or else
he wouldn't move a muscle all day.

This is a poem where dance music
drowns out Sky News. This is a poem
where I sweat and pray at the same time
(and I'm not even naked, or with you),

where the strip-lit room hums with
neighbours and chat and the sweat
or our separate worries, the Holy
Mary mother of God pray for us sinners
now and at the hour of our death amen
kind of sweat, because we won't live
forever but we need to feel blessed,

our dragged bodies and ragged souls
absolved, hands getting slippery
as we puff, all of us bright with worship,

where we remember the communion
of will and muscle, where we remember
how to pray and how to breathe hard.

Brigit (the Accidental Bishop)

Sometimes men do these things, you know.
Forget themselves, lose the run of themselves,
forget that they're supposed to treat women differently
and next thing you know, you've been made a bishop
underneath your wimple and shaved head.

Except you're not allowed to do the day-to-day
rituals because you're a woman—
the sacraments of marriage or birth or death—
so they have to kit you out with a team
of driver-priests to cart you around the country,
baptise the babies for you,
wed the men and women, accompany death.

Everywhere you go, the women greet you
with empty butter churns, casks of water,
sick children and mothers.
You belong to them, and the small tricks
you picked up along the way—
foxglove for fever, Guelder-rose for birth pangs,
a spare bladder of cream in your bag—

spread like folklore up and down the country
until the whispers turn into your name
and the women have claimed you:
poetry under your breath, fire shooting
above your head, mistakes and all.

I Remember My Mother Shaving

I remember my mother shaving. I'd walk past the bathroom door, and there she'd be, leg propped up on the bathtub edge, disposable razor in her right hand. Long, smooth strokes up her shin, against the hair growth. She used to tell me stories about how the other student nurses taught her to shave. Once you started, she said, you couldn't stop. Kind of like Valium or high-sky diving, I guess. When she'd let me have a summertime shower with her—to save money or to save time—I would see that the line of her pubic hair had transformed from a perfect V to a thin strip. I'd look down, waiting for my first hairs to appear.

Her legs were always smooth, so that when she prostrated herself across the altar of her divorce, her family ructions, her homelessness, her legs were hairless before God. What else could she do, and so well? All the gods on earth couldn't hope to achieve such perfection with a razor. She made the men look incompetent. The men, who thought they were gods, would swirl around those smooth, hairless ankles, looking for the secret. All the gods were looking for the secret of smoothness, including my mother. They needed something to make the time pass, something that would help them match each other. Something that would help them be who they were before they ever dreamt of becoming gods.

Leda Revised

There're worse things than being fucked by a swan.
Try going in—a young woman, full of life—
to give birth to your firstborn—that perfect
fleshy egg. Sim-fizz-ee-otomy. I've learnt how to say it,
properly. A slice here, a slice there, my pelvis opens up.
The next day a young nurse teaches me to walk.
Instead of nursing my crying baby I had to learn
to walk again. A big egg, they said, much later. Too big.
Our Lady of Lourdes was worried that if they did one
they'd end up doing ten C-sections on me.
As if my husband wouldn't keep his hands off me—
and not a condom allowed within these holy shores.
They must have pictured me pregnant for decades.
Like I could let him near me again. Pain too strong
to let me hold my baby, even. Waddling everywhere.
Fuckin Zeus. Him and his big shoulders.

Aoibh's Baby Travels to Toronto (Without Her)

I fold your nappies, iron the white dress
stitched when I dreamt of you three rooms
west, ready for your Communion, dressed
in Macroom lace in the house that has no room

for me now. I dress myself first, my hands
pretend to be certain until I whisper your name
out loud. Fionnuala. This name is what I hand
you—hold tight, close your fist around your name.

She Welcomes the World

Here my little *maganda* baby, let me hold
your forehead close enough to smell
the Philippines you left half a world behind,
let me pull you into the warmth of my longing
arms, you are found, you are mine.

Here is the silent space left behind
years ago by our lost brothers and sisters
(they were warbling bundles like you),
babies sent out to find their lives
in Toronto, Boston, Manchester, Melbourne,

following a web of Irish vapour trails.
Let me lose you in my arms, shush now,
you are our brothers and sisters coming home,
wrapped up tight in receiving blankets
borne on the wings of scheduled flights.

Insomnia

I have come to like the hours
spent awake in bed,
the house silent,
everyone else put safely away,
like clean dishes.

The Night Wind

The night wind pulls
at the edges of the house;
a branch grazes my window.
Thoughts flap through my mind
and they land at will.

My mother in a summer dress,
her hand lightly touching my shoulder—
safe—shivers swell up through me,
shivers my spine, shivers my neck,
shivers against her warmth.

My son stirs, calls out for me.
In the middle of the night, I still feel
as though I'm the child.
     So this
is what it's like to be a mother,
to have love expected of you.

I stare into the night room
longing for that sundress.
In the short hours of darkness
I wait for her
to touch my shoulder, again.

Pace Notes

Emily—stuck in the routine
of your home life except to go to prayer meetings—
today I am driving from one house to another,
from the house where I make poetry
to the house where I live
with people I love, where I have to
earn money, wash clothes, hug and cook,
shop and ignore the splashes outside the toilet bowl.
I am a mother, Emily.
I have never lived with a boy before.

Brigit is stuttering—Brigit, my red car,
the original Irish poet—I rev her,
pull through the gates and we're off,
part of me still back with the uneasy thrill
of words, part of me rushing ahead, home.
Potholes and understeer suck me back
into my body, into clutch, pedal, steering wheel,
white knuckles, tap the brakes, drop down a gear
for the bend into Killydoon.

Elizabeth, my co-driver, you would be proud.
Speed camera up ahead, I'm doing 100,
down to 80, your collected poems fly off the seat,
bend to the right
            and hold it hold it hold it
I'm still on the road.
Ignore the dissonance coming from the exhaust,
that's just the critics yakking,
here comes the chicane on the Cavan Road—
lean into the perfect tense, then over again,
Church Ahead (and it's the Feast of the Assumption).
Watch out for the woman fast-walking on the right.

The road is mine, the words are mine,
I am alone in the car, I am car-poet
and yes, I can write childhood memories too,
(like the time my mother reversed into the petrol pump)
and there's a tricky stretch coming up, tight to the white
     line,
          down into third, wide around
the Greek myth in the middle of the road, into 90 left,
watch out for the lyric slipping down from
     the North,
some stony grey soil has fallen off the back of that
     tipper truck.

Two wheels on the tarmac, the rhythm is getting
               away from me,
hold it on the road—I am alone in Brigit, I am nobody—
I grip the steering wheel, steer around the next trochee,
     smooth,
the road is mine Emily, Elizabeth, the words are mine,
it's me and this steering wheel and a line of black tarmac
peeling out of the green ahead;

forget everything I know about driving (just drive!);
right on past Iambic Pentameter, no slowing down now,
watch out for the mongrel at the side of the road
(she looks half-Irish), lost in the notes,
Motorway Ahead, 300 to finish,
almost there—
don't let the poetese slow you down,
don't let the fallen stanzas slow you down,
foot right down, spondees, anapaests, iambs, rhymes
flicking off the windows,
knuckles, nerve, thu-thum, thu-thum,
careening into my prose life
fast,
          and here I am (write it!) flat out—
all the way across the line.

Chainsaw Poem

This afternoon she plucked a yellow chainsaw
from obscurity in Woodies DIY.
'Therapy,' said the woman with the hammer drill.
She couldn't wait to get home, out to the garden,
to heft the chainsaw up to the laurel hedge,
brace her feet against the soggy ground,
rip through the shoots and branches, sculpt
a new family—mother, father, two kids,
Buzz the dog. They don't ask for anything,
they don't complain. They'll outgrow her too
but they can't go anywhere. Her arms shake.
Field maple, boxwood, green privet. Night
sinks in. She can't hear the neighbours complain
over the buzzing of her beloved chainsaw.

Leda Does IVF

Try putting your legs up, opening wide so a doctor
can slide a plastic speculum shaped like a swan's beak
up inside you. Verdicts on the state of your lady bits,
scrapings taken, laser treatments, three weeks of walking
like a cowboy with back trouble. Then injections
and nose sprays, flash sweats and swelling, everywhere.
Six weeks later, it's all worth it. You have two perfect eggs,
swaddled in a Petri dish. Waiting to meet Zeus's
magic seeds, to pit thirty years of science against
the rub of one human cell against another.
Waiting to become something more than myth.

Still

Sarah's poem

This is my baby.
These are her fingers, toes;
stiff. Nothing moves
but my hand, fluttering
across her naked chest.
She is almost perfect
and I whisper breathe,
Anna, mine. My breath
reaches her skin, I am
close, warm, my face
hot with need.

The news goes on. Too much
weather, floods, wind, heat.
Guns discharge straight off
the factory line. More talks.
More truth. A lone woman
stops in the middle of the street,
sings Moon River to throngs.
Customers everywhere.
My feet won't move.

Desire

How can I regret
the parts of me that didn't happen?

The sapling never planted,
the seeds plucked
out of the shallow ground
by wood pigeons or pheasants?

I look down the garden,
see the tops of heads
push up through the soil,
imagine limbs to follow,
ten fingers, ten toes.
Poof. The wind blows,
the clouds move,
the willow branches
tap my window,
insistent as a clock.

Each daughter disappears
as quickly as I can dream her.

Outside My Window

Rain rolls down the glass.
Friends bloom, their bellies swollen
with this spring's soul-crop.

Inside the house, longing thaws.
The cats chase newly-hatched flies.

Heart: Long-term Love Poem

Sometimes it feels like open-heart surgery—
the way I have to approach you gently,
from the side, slice through the layers
of subcutaneous anger, until I get right to it,
there—your ailing heart, a valve that needs
rebuilding, the comm lines clogged up.
I hold your heart in my hands, insert
the stent to keep the blood coursing
through the gloom. You might go on
to thrum another sixteen years with me.
This is too graphic, I know. But here,
I'll say it—I love you even though
it feels as if my ribs have been cracked
open, my chest gaping, your hands
massaging my heart to life (sometimes).

Writing

This is the poem I will write
with my body, reaching
one arm out to feel
the tickle of oxeye daisies
against my palm,
the prick of gravel
under my bare soles,
the test of yeast dough
knuckled under muscle
until it yields, then proves,
springs back under my touch
the way your belly responds
when I wrap myself around you.

Today I will join in the annual
Killanin fun-run and together
we will write bad backs,
arches like wishes,
gimpy ankles, taking shortcuts
past the old graveyard,
both of us setting a jagged pace
until the sprinkle of solid steps
and faltering ones
become part of each other,
part of the road,
until we are thump-muscle,
skin-puddle, eight-year-old girls
overtaking us, until our skin
becomes shiny with effort
and our words threaten
to burst out of our chests.

Turn Left

Murphy's ghost wags his tail
whenever I round the bend.
I follow him through reedy fields,
slip out to the main road,
tracking gentle nose and sense.

He mimes a bark at the cars and I wave,
taunting them with our freedom—
to be able to cut across the bog,
feel dew and brush and squelch,
dance a forgotten prayer.

When our shadows get too long to chase,
we yield to the umbilical pull of home.
Back safe on the low road
a sign reads *Turn left at the black lab*,
for anyone who can see ghosts.

Family

In one hand,
I hold the distant mirage
of my father, in the other,
the times I've picked
fights with my mother.

Countless battles
with at least two sisters
float above my head,
falling slowly towards
my obstinate hands.

But Why

for Sammy

Because you are the only other person I would willingly pick nits from;

because this morning when I shouted *Sit still goddammit* for the third time in thirty seconds I really meant *You are more precious than the clock*;

because even though I didn't find any more nits you will have to sit still again tomorrow for the full hour it takes to check your luxuriant hair;

because sometimes I have to ignore your day's news to finish a poem;

because sometimes I have to refer your complaints to the Official Complaints Department, also known as Later;

because I choose to walk these hill-paths instead of going to town to buy you a new school jumper, because I don't see what's wrong with a patch;

because I am still learning when to close my mouth against the wind and when to let out a bellow;

because lungs, limbs, and a strange thing called consciousness are all I own, and most of the time it feels like they're on loan anyway;

because I am helpless in the reckless embrace of a five-year-old;

because we are fleeting;

because we are here.

Down by the sea

the rock pools have moved—
tides changed, moon waned,
ghost shrimp, white crabs,
other small sea creatures
create new homes, entire villages
within crusted rocks, sea bracken,
sand, a disappearing tide;

the beach is magically transformed.
Yesterday's bed of glistening jellyfish,
babies—not yet old enough
for tentacles or proper tattoos—
have disappeared from the beach,
only a single ink blue one left
stranded on a flat rock, as if it's the only
jellyfish left in the whole world

and it's dead,
flipped over by a man's sole,
but he only did it because
the six-year-old boy pestered him
into revealing the tentacle-free
underside, a bare quivering mass—
'How come it's still moving if it's dead?'
Then he answers his own question,

'Because it's made of jelly'.
Jacques Cousteau Jr we call him,
adventurer and explorer of the shallows,
sea-lover, catcher of dead jellyfish,
dreaming science
under the hot Spiddal sunshine
as if it will be sunny the world over
for ever and ever amen,

the day suspended in heat
and the joy of anemone, sand, crevice,
blue mussel, krill and salty water
that squeezes up your nose and hours later
when you kiss goodnight you can taste
salt and dulse, sea-perfume, sea-condiment,
and you tell me (and I agree)
that this is the best day ever—

a heart beat—so far,
and you repeat it again
(with six years of emphasis)
in case I have missed it,
been distracted by one of the cats
or yet another book—
this is the best day ever,
so far.

Son

Your breath sounds like the ocean
crashing into the shore—constant—
a sound I constantly listen for.
Huff phew,
huff phew,
huff phew.

Sometimes I fear I have imagined you,
breathed life into a wooden puppet
or conjured up a seven-year-old boy
to jump out of a hot skillet
into the bare rooms of my life.

but tonight, your curled warm body
against mine, 3am and night terrors
in another room, I trust your breath,
its proximity, that I will hear the surf
of your story unfurling.

I follow the sound of your breath
to the safety of half a night's sleep,
softly argue with you in my dreams,
huff phew,
huff phew.
Huff phew.

For a Rock at Dog's Bay

You stay put, worn down
by the worship of saltwater
till you become unrecognisable
to your younger self.
Now, the least of you floats above
the sea-hug, even at low tide.
You used to soar upwards.

The sea swishes against
your granite curves, part-secret;
you get used to it, that thrum,
then one swell—and crash!
It's as if you have just met.

Time and relentless lick. Tide after tide.
The kind of steady touch
that doesn't let you think of yourself,
that gives grains of you for miles around,
deposits parts of you hither and thither
until a beach exists, clasts mingled
with the dead bones of fish, the coral sand.

Your Oceans

Ice forms in the coldest part of the stratosphere,
layer by layer—water crystallises drop by drop,
filters down through the clouds to your eyes.

If I could fly up into an expanse of sky
I would choose your blue sky—blue veins
running a course across your broad body,
the heat held safe under your surface.

Show me the border that marks your oceans,
show me your blackweed, your uncharted scars.
If I plunged my hand over the edge of the boat
would you pull me under?

While Vacuuming

The forgetting of being is easy to imagine while cleaning the house again. It starts with stuff. Moves on to mops and buckets and dustcloths. Cream cleaner and bleach, or bicarbonate of soda and vinegar. Vacuuming up flakes of skin and fluff and grit. Bits of yourself and other people.

1

I remember when my baby discovered his toes—he wouldn't let go of them, pulled at them, put them in his mouth. It seems a sense of being precedes any ideas of how a being exists. But I can't really remember when my baby became real. Not during pregnancy anyway. Even the scientific certainty of the sonogram, the pitter pitter pitter of that tiny heartbeat, even the ultrasound scan with its curled-up spine and alien-like head didn't prompt me. My body was mine, after all, no matter what extra sounds it made or pictures they showed me. Even when they handed him into my arms after twelve hours of exhausting work, he didn't seem to exist. When, then, did he become real?

It must have been the first time he cried, and I was the one who had to feed him. That was when we first encountered Heisenberg's uncertainty principle. We've been living it ever since, balanced delicately between knowing who one of us is, and in that moment, the other being impossible to measure.

2

Ten years on, and I discover his dirty socks in the most unlikely places. The theory that no random, spontaneous, mysterious, or miraculous events occur becomes believable when I'm vacuuming the same patch of floor ten years later. I know the surface of my floor better than I know my own naked planes and curves. Every knot, every scratch, every worn-away patch. I am the hero of the vacuum cleaner, I am vac-woman. Sometimes I wish I could assume my mother's approach to cleaning— material objects do not exist unless perceived, and then only as perceptions. If you don't see it, there's no need to clean it.

3

Do dustmites have a will to live? Does the universe living inside my mattress have a will to live? And really, do humans even have a will to live? Would we really drain our world of the very resources that sustain us, if we did? Or are we programmed to acquire, accumulate, appropriate, gain control of pretty much anything that could eventually, possibly, be useful? I look around the house at all the stuff I have collected. This place would be much easier to clean if I chucked most of it. Then I could do what Granny did in her three-roomed thatch cottage: empty the whole house out on a sunny Saturday, scrub every inch—mind and body both stretched along between birth and death—working to become her own hero.

Gym Poem #3

Latimuss Dorsi

As I stretch my arms up over my head
the sensors in my back adjust my stance.
On the wall in front of me, the chart of muscles
shows the groupings I use to balance.

My favourite:

a pair of vast wing-like muscles
splayed across the back as if
we're simply featherless bipeds,
our bird-like nature hidden under our skin.

Moving Red Dot

Armpit waft, freckles, slippery handrail.
Three stage fare. I clasp the carrier bag
to my half-chest as the carriage rocks
against my pulse, hush-swoosh, hush-swoosh.

I am nowhere—not missed, not needed,
a moving red dot on Google Maps.
The backs of my thighs stick to the seat.
I'm off to the beach to forget myself,
my shrinking life: years squeezed into
jobzone eatzone TVzone
                    until life seems silly,

the way a word loses sense
when you repeat it over and over—
armpit armpit armpit—train huddle,
beach sprawl, the smell of Shankill
through the open doors, one more stop
and everyone will slip off,

try on Bray Head, sky open above
our scalps, sea clutter, limbs, our selves
stretched out,
                    ready to lift off.

Notes

OH CANADA—*Câline de bine* (pronounced call-een-de-been) is a French-Canadian minced oath, like saying 'darn it'.

STOP THE LIGHTS—This was the catchphrase of an Irish quiz show called 'Quicksilver' that ran from 1965 to 1981. The phrase was absorbed into Hiberno-English as an interjection of disbelief or exasperation.

EARTH STUDIES—*Cillíní* were the unofficial burial sites for stillborn and un-baptised infants who were considered unsuitable for burial in consecrated ground in Ireland from Early Christian times up to the 20th century.

DEEPWATER HORIZON WIDOW—Eleven men went missing from the oil-drilling platform Deepwater Horizon, in the Gulf of Mexico, as a result of an explosion on 20 April, 2010. Their bodies have never been found, but all are presumed dead.

WHY DO YOU PAWN THINGS RATHER THAN SELL?—A found poem, from 'The Pawn King' episode of 'First Cut', broadcast 14th February 2011 on Channel Four.

THE HOUSE THAT PETER BUILT—Inspired by a story about a long-empty house near the author's home.

UNIVERSAL UTERUS—The images in this poem were inspired by Biosphere2, the first mission to live in a self-sustaining sealed environment that lasted two years from September 1991 in Arizona, USA. An important source for this poem was an article that appeared in the Guardian newspaper on 29/05/2011, written by Adam Curtis, entitled "How the 'ecosystem' myth has been used for sinister means".

BRIGIT (the Accidental Bishop)—Tells the story of Saint Brigit of Kildare.

LEDA REVISED—A symphysiotomy is a surgical procedure (cutting through the symphysis pubis) used to facilitate delivery during childbirth. It is usually only performed in situations where a caesarean section is not an option, as there can be lifelong complications (such as severe pain, incontinence and impaired mobility). In Ireland, an estimated 1,500 women underwent symphysiotomies without consent between 1944 and 1992. A 2012 report found that Our Lady of Lourdes Hospital in Drogheda was carrying out the procedure until the early 1980s.

The poem was written in response to Yeats' sonnet 'Leda and the Swan' about the Greek myth where Zeus takes the form of a swan and either seduces or rapes Leda.

AOIBH'S BABY TRAVELS TO TORONTO (Without Her)—The Irish name 'Aoibh' is pronounced 'Eve'. From the 1940s until the early 1970s an unknown number of Irish children born to unwed mothers were sent abroad by Catholic organisations, for adoption.

SHE WELCOMES—'maganda' is Filipino for beautiful.

PACE NOTES—Composed on the drive back from the Tyrone Guthrie Centre (an artists' retreat in County Monaghan).

Visit www.celesteauge.com for more information about the author, or to contact her to request a poetry reading or interview.

CELESTE AUGÉ is the author of *The Essential Guide to Flight* (Salmon Poetry, 2009) and the collection of short stories *Fireproof and Other Stories* (Doire Press, 2012). *The World Literature Review* has said: 'Celeste Augé's poems are commendable for their care, deep thought, and intellectual ambition.'

She works in the area of adult education, teaching creative writing to undergraduates at NUI Galway as well as tutoring with a local Adult Learning Centre.

Celeste has a Masters degree in writing from NUI Galway. Her poetry has been short-listed for a Hennessy Award, and she received a Literature Bursary from the Arts Council of Ireland to write *Skip Diving*. In 2011, she won the Cúirt New Writing Prize for fiction. She lives in Connemara, in the West of Ireland, with her husband and son.